THE BOOK OF

Isaiah 1~23

ONE CHAPTER A DAY

GoodMorningGirls.org

The Book of Isaiah 1-23

© 2020 Women Living Well Ministries, LLC

ALL RIGHTS RESERVED

Welcome to Good Morning Girls! We are so glad you are joining us.

God created us to walk with Him, to know Him, and to be loved by Him. He is our living well, and when we drink from the water He continually provides, His living water will change the entire course of our lives.

Jesus said: "Whoever drinks of the water that I will give him will never be thirsty again. The water that I will give him will become in him a spring of water welling up to eternal life." ~ John 4:14 (ESV)

So let's begin.

• no assigned passages
• Some may not SOAK at all
• Some may SOAK more verses or write out the entire chapter

The method we use here at GMG is called the **SOAK** method.

- **S**—The S stands for *Scripture*—Read the chapter for the day. Then choose 1-2 verses and write them out word for word. (There is no right or wrong choice— just let the Holy Spirit guide you.)

- **O**—The O stands for *Observation*—Look at the verse or verses you wrote out. Write 1 or 2 observations. What stands out to you? What do you learn about the character of God from these verses? Is there a promise, command or teaching?

- **A**—The A stands for *Application*—Personalize the verses. What is God saying to you? How can you apply them to your life? Are there any changes you need to make or an action to take?
  my one word!

- **K**—The K stands for *Kneeling in Prayer*—Pause, kneel and pray. Confess any sin God has revealed to you today. Praise God for His word. Pray the passage over your own life or someone you love. Ask God to help you live out your applications.

SOAK God's word into your heart and squeeze every bit of nourishment you can out of each day's scripture reading. Soon you will find your life transformed by the renewing of your mind!

Walk with the King!

Courtney

WomenLivingWell.org, GoodMorningGirls.org

Join the GMG Community

Share your daily SOAK on **Facebook.com/GoodMorningGirlsWLW**

Instagram: WomenLivingWell #GoodMorningGirls

GMG Bible Coloring Chart

COLORS	KEYWORDS
PURPLE	God, Jesus, Holy Spirit, Saviour, Messiah
PINK	women of the Bible, family, marriage, parenting, friendship, relationships
RED	love, kindness, mercy, compassion, peace, grace
GREEN	faith, obedience, growth, fruit, salvation, fellowship, repentance
YELLOW	worship, prayer, praise, doctrine, angels, miracles, power of God, blessings
BLUE	wisdom, teaching, instruction, commands
ORANGE	prophecy, history, times, places, kings, genealogies, people, numbers, covenants, vows, visions, oaths, future
BROWN/GRAY	Satan, sin, death, hell, evil, idols, false teachers, hypocrisy, temptation

Introduction to the Book of Isaiah

The name Isaiah means *salvation is of the Lord*. Isaiah brought to Israel and Judah, a message of judgement for their rebellion but also a message of hope for salvation, through the coming Messiah.

For the first part of Isaiah, Isaiah focuses on God's judgement of Israel. Isaiah's message is one of condemnation for their faithless rebellion against God. God's people had turned their back on God and had become like the other nations around them. God would use the Assyrians and Babylonians to bring judgement upon them. Isaiah called on God's people to turn back and seek the Lord and he assures them that after judgement, a godly remnant would remain.

For the second part of Isaiah, Isaiah announces that Israel's punishment and exile is over, and salvation has come. We see that God is faithful to his covenant promises. No other prophet is quoted in the New Testament as much as Isaiah. Isaiah foretold the coming King of Israel, who would rule in justice and peace and would bear their sins.

The book of Isaiah offers the most complete prophetic picture of Jesus Christ in the entire Old Testament. Some of the prophecies fulfilled in Christ from the book of Isaiah are: he would be born of a virgin (Isaiah 7:14), he would be spit on and struck (Isaiah 50:6), he would be disfigured by suffering (Isaiah 52:14; 53:2), he would be rejected (Isaiah 53:1-3), he would bear our sins (Isaiah 53:4-5, 12), he would voluntarily die like a lamb to the slaughter (Isaiah 53:7), he would heal the blind, lame, deaf, diseased, broken hearted and raise from the dead (Isaiah 26:19, Isaiah 29:18-19, Isaiah 61:1-2) he would be buried in a rich man's tomb (Isaiah 53:9) and he would return to claim his own (Isaiah 60:2-3). Because of all of these prophecies fulfilled in Christ, this book is a book of hope and salvation from the Lord.

The Purpose: God used Isaiah to proclaim judgement to his people, so they would repent and turn back to him. He also used Isaiah's message of coming hope and salvation, to be a comfort to them.

The Author: Isaiah was a well-educated prophet, who was married, with two children. Tradition holds that Isaiah was martyred by being sawn in two. Isaiah ministered during the reign of Uzziah, Jotham, Ahaz and Hezekiah. Isaiah was a contemporary to the prophets Hosea and Micah. More about Israel's history during this time period can be found in 2 Kings 15-21 and 2 Chronicles 26-33.

Time Period: 740-680 B.C.

Key Verse: Isaiah 12:2

> *Behold, God is my salvation;*
> *I will trust, and will not be afraid;*
> *for the Lord God is my strength and my song,*
> *and he has become my salvation.*

The Outline:

Message of Judgement (1-35)

- The coming judgement of Israel and Judah (1-5)
- Isaiah's calling (6-7)
- Judgement and hope (8-12)
- Judgement of the other nations (13-24)
- Promised restoration (25-27)
- Judgement and salvation (28-35)

Isaiah and Hezekiah (36-39)

- Messages of Comfort and Salvation (40-66)
- The Lord's plan of restoration for Israel (40-45)
- The fall of Babylon (46-48)
- Salvation through the servant (49-56)
- Call to repentance (57-59)
- Glorious salvation (60-65)
- God's righteous and final judgement (66)

Despite God giving Israel multiple chances to repent and turn from their ways, they continued in their sin and rebellion. As a result, God's judgement was upon them. But even through all of the dark times, God was still at work among His people. Eventually, salvation would come through the Messiah. God keeps his covenant promises to his people. We serve a faithful God, who loves us.

So, let's get started studying His word! Some of the chapters are quite long, so be sure to leave at least 20 minutes for your reading each day. I can't wait to see how God reveals himself personally to each of us, as we read the book of Isaiah together, chapter by chapter.

Keep walking with the King!

Courtney

Come now, let us reason together,

says the Lord:

though your sins are like scarlet,

they shall be as white as snow.

Isaiah 1:18

Reflection Question:

In Isaiah 1:1, the word vision means a revelation from God. This entire book is a revelation from God through Isaiah, for Israel. As the book of Isaiah opens, God calls on heaven and earth to be a witness of Israel's sin. God does not want their religious rituals; he wants their hearts, but their hearts are far from him. And so, God invites his people to reason with him. He wants them to see the love he has for them, as he offers to make their sins that are like scarlet, as white as snow.

Jesus died on the cross for our sins. When we place our faith in him, the stain of sin is removed. Have you ever considered that it is reasonable to follow God? Many think it is foolish to follow God, but when we consider the infinite wisdom, love, grace and power of God, we cannot help but to follow him. Are you struggling right now with any shame, guilt, or pain from sin in your past? How does remembering the truth—that though your sins were as scarlet, God has made them as white as snow—comfort you?

Isaiah 1

S—The S stands for *Scripture*

O—The O stands for *Observation*

A—The A stands for *Application*

K—The K stands for *Kneeling in Prayer*

Come, let us walk

in the light of the Lord.

Isaiah 2:5

Reflection Question:

Israel was walking in darkness. They were trusting in their own strength, their own horses and their own chariots. They were bowing down to idols and adopting the practices of other nations, such as fortune telling and greed. In the latter days, his people will return to him and Israel will rise above the other nations.

God's people were living in chaos, rebellion and darkness. But we do not have to live in darkness, God sent his son to be the light of the world! He is the way, the truth and the life. We do not have to wait, for the latter days, to walk in the light of the Lord. That invitation is for us now. How is Jesus your light and what blessings have you experienced from walking in the light of the Lord?

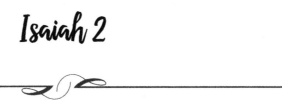

S—The S stands for *Scripture*

O—The O stands for *Observation*

A—The A stands for *Application*

K—The K stands for *Kneeling in Prayer*

Tell the righteous

that it shall be well with them,

for they shall eat the fruit of their deeds.

Isaiah 3:10

Reflection Question:

God brought judgement on Judah and Jerusalem because they had sinned in their words and deeds and they had defied God's presence. So, God took away their bread, water, soldiers, judges, prophets and leaders. Next came social division, as the rich were against the poor and the young against the old. All this evil, they had brought upon themselves.

Israel had no shame as they defied God and so God disciplined them, but everything was well with the righteous. In the midst of those living in rebellion to God, there will always be the faithful few that God will bless and protect. And even though the righteous suffer here on earth, in eternity, we will be rewarded for our faithfulness. Are you living in righteousness? How does knowing that you do not share the same fate as the wicked, encourage you?

S—The S stands for *Scripture*

O—The O stands for *Observation*

A—The A stands for *Application*

K—The K stands for *Kneeling in Prayer*

And he who is left in Zion

and remains in Jerusalem

will be called holy.

Isaiah 4:3

Reflection Question:

When Isaiah refers to the branch of the Lord, he is speaking of the promise of the coming Messiah. After the cleansing of the unfaithful from Israel, a holy remnant will be left in Jerusalem. Isaiah says, when the branch of the Lord reigns, he will lead them by a cloud in the day and a flaming fire by night and the presence of the Lord will be with them.

God sought to purify Israel and make them holy. Holy means to be set apart for the Lord. As a believer, you have been declared holy and set apart for the Lord's use. Do you find it hard to live a holy life, when you are surrounded by a world that embraces sin and ungodly living? How is your lifestyle different from an unbeliever's lifestyle?

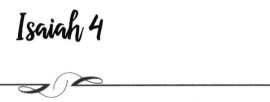

S—The S stands for *Scripture*

O—The O stands for *Observation*

A—The A stands for *Application*

K—The K stands for *Kneeling in Prayer*

Woe to those who call evil good

and good evil,

who put darkness for light

and light for darkness.

Isaiah 5:20

Reflection Question:

Isaiah begins this chapter singing a love song about a vineyard that grew wild grapes. Because the grapes were wild, the Lord destroyed the vineyard, which was a picture of Israel. Then, Isaiah listed 6 woes or 6 sins that brought the judgement of God upon them, which included calling evil good and good evil.

The word "woe" is an expression of deep distress, as an inescapable judgement is about to come. It is also used in scriptures as a way to express grief, regret, or the condition of deep suffering. Since the Garden of Eden, Satan has been making evil appear good and good appear evil and this is very dangerous. How do you see this in the world around you right now? Is there an area in your life, where you are tempted to call evil good and good evil?

Isaiah 5

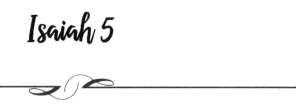

S—The S stands for *Scripture*

O—The O stands for *Observation*

A—The A stands for *Application*

K—The K stands for *Kneeling in Prayer*

I saw the Lord

sitting upon a throne,

high and lifted up;

and the train of his robe

filled the temple.

Isaiah 6:1

Reflection Question:

King Uzziah was a good king and in the year that he died, Isaiah saw the Lord sitting on his throne, high and lifted up. Though Israel was being rebellious to God, God was still on this throne. The train of his robe filled the temple. This temple was not the one in Jerusalem but the heavenly temple. The train must have been amazing! Angelic creatures surrounded his throne calling out, "Holy, holy, holy is the Lord of hosts; the whole earth is full of his glory." The temple shook and was filled with smoke.

Pause and take in this majestic view of God. In the midst of all the chaos, where was God? He was still on his throne, in complete control. When Isaiah compared himself to God, he was afraid because of his sinfulness, but then God atoned for his sin and took away his guilt. What a beautiful picture of amazing grace. God has given us this same amazing grace, through his son Jesus. Does the world around you seem chaotic? Is there something you are worried about today? How does seeing God as he is, on his throne reigning in all his glory and authority, bring you peace?

Isaiah 6

S—The S stands for *Scripture*

O—The O stands for *Observation*

A—The A stands for *Application*

K—The K stands for *Kneeling in Prayer*

The Lord himself will give you a sign.

Behold, the virgin shall conceive

and bear a son,

and shall call his name Immanuel.

Isaiah 7:14

Reflection Question:

The prophecy of Isaiah 7:14 is one of the most famous prophecies in the Bible. Matthew 1:22-23 says, "All this took place to fulfill what the Lord had spoken by the prophet: "Behold, the virgin shall conceive and bear a son, and they shall call his name Immanuel (which means, God with us)". So, according to Matthew, the virgin is Mary and the son is Jesus.

Jesus fulfilled the prophecy of Isaiah 7:14. He is both God and man and his deity is what makes him able to be our savior. He is Immanuel - God with us! He came to both live and die, so that we would not have to die, but rather live with him. Do you sometimes feel alone or lonely? When or why do you feel this way? How does remembering that you are never alone, and God is always with you, help you feel less alone?

S—The S stands for *Scripture*

O—The O stands for *Observation*

A—The A stands for *Application*

K—The K stands for *Kneeling in Prayer*

I will wait for the Lord.

Isaiah 8:17

Reflection Question:

The Assyrians were about to invade Judah. As they waited, Isaiah reminded them not to sit and wait on their enemies but instead to wait on the Lord. He wanted them to take their focus off of the Assyrian army and instead focus on God and put their hope in him.

When we are fearful, God wants us to trust in him. Waiting on him means that we will not focus on all the things we fear the most but instead be paying attention to God's every move. Is there something you are afraid of today? How can you shift your thoughts from focusing on the thing you fear most, to focusing on God and putting your hope in him?

S—The S stands for *Scripture*

O—The O stands for *Observation*

A—The A stands for *Application*

K—The K stands for *Kneeling in Prayer*

For to us a child is born, to us a son is given;

and the government shall be upon his shoulder,

and his name shall be called

Wonderful Counselor, Mighty God,

Everlasting Father, Prince of Peace.

Isaiah 9:6

Reflection Question:

Jesus' birth fulfilled this prophecy. He came as both fully God and fully man and his names describe who he is and what he can do. He is a Wonderful Counselor. There is no one more qualified to guide your life than him. He is the Mighty God. He is the one worthy of all worship and praise. He is the Everlasting Father. He has no beginning and no end. He is the Prince of Peace. When we trust in him, he causes our hearts to be at peace.

In what area of your life do you need counsel? Is something stealing your peace today? Write it below and then be still. Remember that Jesus is a Wonderful Counselor and the Prince of Peace. He wants you to come to him with your worries and concerns. He is a mighty God who is with you and loves you. Pray and put your trust in him.

S—The S stands for *Scripture*

O—The O stands for *Observation*

A—The A stands for *Application*

K—The K stands for *Kneeling in Prayer*

Woe to those who

turn aside the needy from justice

and rob the poor of my people of their right.

Isaiah 10:1-2

Reflection Question:

Israel and their leaders had forsaken the poor in their times of need. They had no mercy for the weak. And so, in their times of need, there would be no mercy for them. Without God, they had no protection or strength against their enemies. God used their enemies to judge them. Essentially, Assyria was doing the Lord's work when they went into battle against Israel, Judah and Syria. They were God's instruments of wrath.

In the book of Isaiah, we see the sovereignty of God through fulfilled prophecy in how he uses Israel's enemies to judge them. This shows us how God can use things that seem bad in our lives, for our good. Name a time when you faced painful opposition but later saw the good in it? God cares about how you are treated, and he loves you. Keep trusting in him.

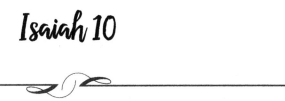

S—The S stands for **Scripture**

O—The O stands for **Observation**

A—The A stands for **Application**

K—The K stands for **Kneeling in Prayer**

And the Spirit of the Lord shall rest upon him,

the Spirit of wisdom and understanding,

the Spirit of counsel and might,

the Spirit of knowledge and the fear of the Lord.

Isaiah 11:2

Reflection Question:

It was foretold that the Messiah would come from the House of Jesse, who was the father of David. And the Spirit of the Lord would be on the Messiah, with a spirit of wisdom, understanding, counsel, might, knowledge and the fear of the Lord.

Jesus is perfect in wisdom and counsel because he understands all things. He has knowledge that we do not have, so his ways are higher than ours. He is all powerful and able to do more than we can ask or imagine. What an amazing savior we have! Jesus knows everything including our thoughts and heart desires -- and he loved us so much, he died for us. How does remembering that Jesus is full of wisdom, understanding, counsel, might, and knowledge, remind you that you have a sympathetic savior, who cares for you?

Isaiah 11

S—The S stands for *Scripture*

O—The O stands for *Observation*

A—The A stands for *Application*

K—The K stands for *Kneeling in Prayer*

27

Behold, God is my salvation;

I will trust, and will not be afraid.

Isaiah 12:2

Reflection Question:

Even though they have felt the wrath of God, this short chapter is full of praise because God is their salvation. They have peace in the midst of turmoil because they have chosen to trust in God. This choice has removed their fear and given them strength, confidence and a song in their hearts.

Some people try to be their own salvation through good works. As a result, life is hard and full of anxiety. But our salvation is through our faith in Jesus' death and resurrection alone. How has your decision to trust in Jesus for your salvation, given you peace and strength? What are you worried about today, that you need to trust God with?

S—The S stands for *Scripture*

O—The O stands for *Observation*

A—The A stands for *Application*

K—The K stands for *Kneeling in Prayer*

Therefore, I will make the heavens tremble,

and the earth will be shaken out of its place,

at the wrath of the Lord of hosts

in the day of his fierce anger.

Isaiah 13:13

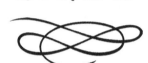

Reflection Question:

Isaiah speaks of the judgement of Babylon, in the day of the Lord. The day of the Lord is more than one day. It's more like a season. This prophecy has a double fulfillment that is both near and far. Isaiah is referring to both the judgement of the Babylonian Empire and the final judgment, when Jesus returns.

When we consider how God can literally shake the heavens and the earth, we are reminded of his great strength and power. Our God is unshakable! We can trust in him more than the ground we walk on. Look out the window now at all God has created. List below a few of the things you see, that remind you of the glory and brilliance of God. Remember that the creator of this universe loves you and you can trust in him. He is a firm foundation to build your life upon.

S—The S stands for *Scripture*

O—The O stands for *Observation*

A—The A stands for *Application*

K—The K stands for *Kneeling in Prayer*

The Lord of hosts has sworn:

"As I have planned, so shall it be,

and as I have purposed, so shall it stand.

Isaiah 14:24

Reflection Question:

God is sovereign. He is all powerful and all that he plans or purposes—will be. We see God's sovereignty woven throughout all of the book of Isaiah, as prophecies are fulfilled, and nations are brought low. Nothing can stop God. He is sovereign over all of nature and all the nations. What he says he will do—he does.

Because God is full of wisdom, justice and mercy, we can trust in God's plan. We do not have to fear what our future holds, because we know who holds the future. How does God's sovereignty bring you comfort and in what area of your life do you need to trust God more?

S—The S stands for *Scripture*

O—The O stands for *Observation*

A—The A stands for *Application*

K—The K stands for *Kneeling in Prayer*

My heart cries out for Moab.

Isaiah 15:5

Reflection Question:

Isaiah saw how devastating the judgement of God was about to be on the people of Moab and he lamented. The Moabites had always been enemies of Israel but King David's grandmother, Ruth, was a Moabite. This meant that King David himself was one-fourth Moabite. The pain that Moab would experience would be seen by all. God would complete his judgement, and none would escape. So this caused Isaiah to experience sadness on their behalf.

Though the Moabites were enemies of Israel, Isaiah notably had empathy toward them in their distress. In Matthew 5:44, Jesus tells us to love our enemies and to pray for those who persecute us. Who is someone you would consider an enemy in your life? How can you have a more tender spirit toward them? Write a prayer below for your enemy and release them to the Lord.

Isaiah 15

S—The S stands for *Scripture*

O—The O stands for *Observation*

A—The A stands for *Application*

K—The K stands for *Kneeling in Prayer*

We have heard of the pride of Moab—

how proud he is!—

of his arrogance, his pride, and his insolence;

in his idle boasting he is not right.

Isaiah 16:6

Reflection Question:

Isaiah reveals that the sin of Moab is their pride. They took great glory in their vineyards and so God was about to destroy all their vineyards. The prophet's heart continued to mourn for them because he could see that they were seeking joy and fulfillment in all the wrong places. Isaiah concludes this chapter by warning the Moabites that within 3 years, all of this devastating judgement would take place.

It is interesting to note that Moab's sin was pride because they were not a mighty nation like Assyria or Babylon. This reminds us that we are all susceptible to the temptation of pride, whether we are great in the world's eyes or not. Reflect on your own life now. Is there an area in your life where pride has crept in? When was the last time you bragged about something big or small to someone else? God has a way of humbling us when we go too far with our pride. So, rather than facing God's humbling discipline, confess that pride now to the Lord.

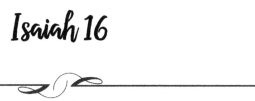

S—The S stands for *Scripture*

O—The O stands for *Observation*

A—The A stands for *Application*

K—The K stands for *Kneeling in Prayer*

In that day
man will look to his Maker,
and his eyes will look
on the Holy One of Israel.

Isaiah 17:7

Reflection Question:

Damascus was the beautiful capital city of Syria and God was about to bring them down to a heap of ruins. As a result of the coming judgement, some would respond and turn back to the Lord. God used the destruction of their wooden images, altars and strong cities to turn them back to himself. This fulfills the purpose of God's judgement.

When we begin to go astray and trust in the things of this world, that is not best for us. So, sometimes God will remove the things we are trusting in, to turn our focus back to him. Has God ever removed something from your life so that you would be more focused on him? Who or what are you trusting in today? Is there anything that you are depending on more than God?

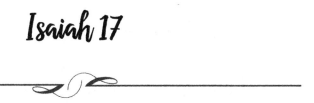

S—The S stands for *Scripture*

O—The O stands for *Observation*

A—The A stands for *Application*

K—The K stands for *Kneeling in Prayer*

For thus the Lord said to me:

"I will quietly look from my dwelling

like clear heat in sunshine,

like a cloud of dew in the heat of harvest."

Isaiah 18:4

Reflection Question:

God sees all from his dwelling place. Nothing is kept a secret from him. He patiently waits in stillness, as he observes the nations. His good presence is welcomed by his people, like the heat of sunshine after the rain, that causes plants to flourish. His presence is also like a cloud of dew in the heat of harvest. The dew refreshes the ground and the cloud is a blessing to the workers.

God protects and cares for his people in all seasons of life. Does the Lord seem silent or slow in your life right now? He has not left you alone. He sees you. At just the right time, he will move in your life. Often times, we cannot see the moves he is making, until we look back with a better perspective. Think of a time when God seemed still or silent but later you were able to see that he was watching over you and taking care of you. How was he at work in your life during that time?

S—The S stands for *Scripture*

O—The O stands for *Observation*

A—The A stands for *Application*

K—The K stands for *Kneeling in Prayer*

When they cry to the Lord
because of oppressors,
he will send them a savior
and defender and deliver them.

Isaiah 19:20

Reflection Question:

Oppression caused the Egyptians to cry out to God for help and God heard their cries. He said he would send a savior and defender to deliver them. This prophecy was fulfilled through Christ, the savior of the world, who delivers us from our sin.

Jesus is our savior and defender. He delivers us from the oppression of sin. To be oppressed is to be under the control of something or to be in distress because of the authority and power something or someone has over you. Have you ever felt oppressed by your own sin? What caused you to feel this way and how is Jesus your savior and defender?

Isaiah 19

S—The S stands for *Scripture*

O—The O stands for *Observation*

A—The A stands for *Application*

K—The K stands for *Kneeling in Prayer*

At that time the Lord spoke by Isaiah

the son of Amoz, saying,

"Go..."

Isaiah 20:2

Reflection Question:

Sometimes God asked his prophets to use visible signs to help his people understand their warnings. So, God gave Isaiah an assignment to live for three years unclothed, as a sign to Judah to not look to Egypt to protect them from Assyria. Some say that Isaiah removed his outer garment but would have still had on his undergarments. The point was that he would be dressed as one who is poor and destitute and in great need of help.

Sometimes we look for security in all the wrong places. Perhaps we look for it in a person, a place, a thing or our bank account. When we trust in the temporal things of this earth, we inevitably end up disappointed. Sure, temporarily they bring security but nothing here on earth is for sure. The one thing that is always guaranteed is change. There is no firm foundation or security in life except in the Lord. What or who do you lean on for security in life? Has this person or thing taken the place of God in your life? How can you trust in God more today?

S—The S stands for *Scripture*

O—The O stands for *Observation*

A—The A stands for *Application*

K—The K stands for *Kneeling in Prayer*

For the Lord,

the God of Israel,

has spoken.

Isaiah 21:17

Reflection Question:

When God speaks, it happens. In verse 9, it says *"Fallen, fallen is Babylon."* We see this same repetition and phrase used in Revelation 18:1-2. It reads, *"After this I saw another angel coming down from heaven. He had great authority, and the earth was illuminated by his splendor. 2 With a mighty voice he shouted:"* *'Fallen! Fallen is Babylon the Great!'*

The same fear and trembling that took place when Babylon fell the first time, will also take place one day when God judges the world. We see in Revelation 18:9-19, the world mourning the loss of Babylon. But in Revelation 18:20, God's people rejoice over the judgement of Babylon.

If you have a minute, flip over to Revelation 18, you will see that Babylon is a city filled with pride, greed, and self-indulgence. They are a commercial society of buying and selling. Their sins are great and so a swift judgement will come upon them by the mighty judge, God. Reflect on your life for a moment. Does the commercialism or materialism of this world's system tempt you? Do you ever struggle with materialism, pride, greed or self-indulgence? Confess it to the Lord now.

S—The S stands for *Scripture*

O—The O stands for *Observation*

A—The A stands for *Application*

K—The K stands for *Kneeling in Prayer*

And I will place on his shoulder

the key of the house of David.

He shall open, and none shall shut;

and he shall shut, and none shall open.

Isaiah 22:22

Reflection Question:

This passage speaks of the Lord giving authority to his servant, Eliakim. But it is also a prophecy of Jesus, who holds the keys to death and Hades. (Rev. 1:18) This is evident by Isaiah 22:22 being quoted in Revelation 3:7. It says, "The words of the holy one, the true one, who has the key of David, who opens, and no one will shut, who shuts, and no one opens."

Our loving God is sovereign overall. His plan cannot be thwarted. This should be a great comfort to us but sometimes, it is hard to wait on God to open doors. In the entryway of my home, there is a picture hanging on the wall that reads: "Until God opens the next door, praise him in the hallway." Are you in a season of waiting on God to open a door for you right now? Has he ever closed a door that you wish he had left open? How can you trust God more with his open and closed doors?

Isaiah 22

S—The S stands for *Scripture*

O—The O stands for *Observation*

A—The A stands for *Application*

K—The K stands for *Kneeling in Prayer*

The Lord of hosts has purposed it.

Isaiah 23:9

Reflection Question:

In the city of Tyre, the merchants and traders were successful businessmen and they became the rulers. They were given great power, honor, influence and fame. They were treated like princes. As a result, God purposed to bring judgement upon them because of their pride. God's judgement was measured to the exact number of 70 years. What the Lord purposes to do—he will do.

The desire for wealth can be a trap, when it is used for self-glory rather than God's glory. Where there is greed, there is envy, selfishness, and pride. Greed always wants more and is never satisfied. Jesus warns us in Luke 12:15, ""Watch out! Be on your guard against all kinds of greed; life does not consist in an abundance of possessions." Life is not about our possessions. Having money and wealth is not a sin but money is a poor substitute for God. We must not put our trust in money. Has greed or selfishness crept into your life? What have you learned about the character of God, in Isaiah chapters one through twenty-three, that leads you trust God more with everything in your life?

S—The S stands for *Scripture*

O—The O stands for *Observation*

A—The A stands for *Application*

K—The K stands for *Kneeling in Prayer*

Made in the USA
Coppell, TX
15 January 2021